LET'S LEARN NOUNS!

BIRD!

BY KATE MIKOLEY

 Gareth Stevens
PUBLISHING

Please visit our website, www.garethstevens.com. For a free color catalog of all our high-quality books, call toll free 1-800-542-2595 or fax 1-877-542-2596.

Cataloging-in-Publication Data

Names: Mikoley, Kate.
Title: Let's learn nouns! / Kate Mikoley.
Description: New York : Gareth Stevens Publishing, 2019. | Series: Wonderful world of words | Includes glossary and index.
Identifiers: LCCN ISBN 9781538218891 (pbk.) | ISBN 9781538218877 (library bound) | ISBN 9781538218907 (6 pack)
Subjects: LCSH: English language–Noun–Juvenile literature.
Classification: LCC PE1201.M54 2019 | DDC 428.2–dc23

Published in 2019 by
Gareth Stevens Publishing
111 East 14th Street, Suite 349
New York, NY 10003

Copyright © 2019 Gareth Stevens Publishing

Designer: Katelyn E. Reynolds
Editor: Emily Mahoney

Photo credits: Cover, p. 1 Dave Nelson/Shutterstock.com; p. 5 (dog) Monika Chodak/Shutterstock.com; p. 5 (apple) Alex Staroseltsev/Shutterstock.com; p. 5 (pencil) Sarawut Aiemsinsuk/Shutterstock.com; p. 5 (house) romakoma/Shutterstock.com; p. 7 Newman Studio/Shutterstock.com; p. 9 Eric Cote/Shutterstock.com; p. 11 Harvepino/Shutterstock.com; p. 13 Monkey Business Images/Shutterstock.com; p. 15 michaeljung/Shutterstock.com; p. 17 bondvit/Shutterstock.com; p. 19 plantic/Shutterstock.com; p. 21 Rawpixel.com/Shutterstock.com.

Printed in the United States of America

CPSIA compliance information: Batch #CS18GS: For further information contact Gareth Stevens, New York, New York at 1-800-542-2595.

CONTENTS

Boldface words appear in the glossary.

Neat Nouns

What do the words *dog*, *apple*, *house*, and *pencil* have in common? They're all nouns! A noun is a word that is the name of something. People, places, and things are nouns. Read on to learn more about them. Check your answers on page 22!

Common Nouns

Words such as *school* or *cat* are called common nouns. Common nouns are general words for people, places, or things. Can you spot the common noun in the sentence below?

Sam walked down the street.

Proper Nouns

The names of **specific** people, places, or things are called proper nouns. Your name is a proper noun. However, the words *child*, *boy*, and *girl* are common nouns. Find the proper noun in the following sentence:

Sara plays soccer at school.

Proper nouns aren't just the names of people. They're also the names of places. *Sweden* is a proper noun. However, the word *country* is a common noun. Proper nouns are capitalized. Common nouns usually aren't.

Sweden

Subjects and Objects

In a sentence, nouns are often the subject or object of a **verb**. The subject is the noun that's doing the action of the verb. The object is the noun that receives the verb's action. Which noun is the subject of the following sentence?

Joe rides the bus.

All Kinds of Nouns

People's names are nouns. So are their jobs. For example, if your teacher's name is Ms. Smith, you could use the noun *teacher* to talk about her. You could also use her name. Find the two nouns below.

My doctor is named Dr. Jones.

A Ferrari is an **expensive** kind of car. They're known for going very fast. Since it's the name of the company, *Ferrari* is a proper noun.

Car and *truck* are also nouns. What kind of nouns are these words?

People, places, and things that you can touch, hear, or see are called **concrete** nouns. Some nouns are things you can't touch, like feelings or ideas. These are called **abstract** nouns. *Love* is an abstract noun. So are *anger* and *happiness*.

So Many Nouns

Nouns are all around us. If you look around your classroom or backyard, you can probably find a lot of them! Look at the picture on the next page. How many nouns can you name?

THE CHICKEN
LIFE CYCLE

GLOSSARY

abstract: a thought or idea that isn't connected to an object

concrete: having to do with specific people or things rather than general ideas

expensive: costing a lot of money

specific: exact

verb: an action word

ANSWER KEY

p. 6: street

p. 8: Sara

p. 12: Joe

p. 14: doctor, Dr. Jones

p. 16: common nouns

FOR MORE INFORMATION

BOOKS

Ayers, Linda. *Farmers, Firefighters, and Teachers: They Are Nouns!* North Mankato, MN: Cantata Learning, 2017.

Doyle, Sheri. *What Is a Noun?* North Mankato, MN: Capstone Press, 2013.

Murray, Kara. *Nouns and Pronouns.* New York, NY: PowerKids Press, 2014.

WEBSITES

Grammar Gorillas
www.funbrain.com/games/grammar-gorillas
Find the nouns and other parts of speech in this fun game.

Nouns and Verbs
www.abcya.com/nouns_and_verbs.htm
This game will help you learn more about nouns and find out about verbs, too!

The Noun
www.chompchomp.com/terms/noun.htm
Learn more about nouns here!

Publisher's note to educators and parents: Our editors have carefully reviewed these websites to ensure that they are suitable for students. Many websites change frequently, however, and we cannot guarantee that a site's future contents will continue to meet our high standards of quality and educational value. Be advised that students should be closely supervised whenever they access the internet.

INDEX

5